# RIGHT
# STANDING
## *with*
# GOD

## *Study Guide*

## KENNETH
## COPELAND

# RIGHT STANDING
## *with*
# GOD

*Study Guide*

# KENNETH COPELAND

KENNETH COPELAND
PUBLICATIONS

*Right-Standing With God*
Study Guide

ISBN-10 1-57562-657-8                     30-0719
ISBN-13 978-1-57562-657-4

24 23 22 21 20 19                          10 9 8 7 6 5

© 1983 International Church of the Word of Faith Inc. now known as Eagle Mountain International Church Inc. aka Kenneth Copeland Ministries

Kenneth Copeland Ministries
Fort Worth, TX  76192-0001

For more information about Kenneth Copeland Ministries, visit kcm.org or call 1-800-600-7395 (U.S. only) or +1-817-852-6000.

# 1

# "Seek ye first the kingdom of God, and his righteousness...."

Matthew 6:33

To *seek* means "to acquire or gain."
What does gaining God's kingdom
and His righteousness mean to us
in the challenges of everyday life?

## MESSAGE ONE

### Seek First the Kingdom I

## Focus on What's Most Important...Everything Else Will Fall Into Place

"*T*herefore take no thought, saying, What shall we eat? or, What shall we drink? or, Wherewithal shall we be clothed?...for your heavenly Father knoweth that ye have need of all these things. But seek ye first the kingdom of God, and his righteousness; and all these things shall be added unto you."

Matthew 6:31-33

# You Can Walk Free From Worry and the Power of Sin

**FOCUS:** "[God] hath delivered us from the power of darkness, and hath translated us into the kingdom of his dear Son" (Colossians 1:13).

To *seek* means "to try to acquire or gain." The Word tells us to seek first the kingdom of God and His righteousness (Matthew 6:33). We must first know what these are, to be able to acquire or gain them.

Colossians 1:13 says that we, as believers, have been delivered from the power of darkness and translated into the kingdom of God's dear Son. Jesus is an heir of God. He said everything the Father has is His.

Romans 8:17 calls us heirs of God and joint heirs with Christ—everything the Father has is ours.

Through our union with Christ at the new birth, we are no longer subject to Satan's dominion. The law of the Spirit of life in Christ Jesus has made us free from the law of sin and death (Romans 8:2).

The realm of the spirit in which God operates, is available to us. Therefore, to seek after the kingdom of God is to seek after the things of God.

Jesus said, "My kingdom is not of this world." He said that the kingdom of God is within you (Luke 17:21). He was speaking of your spirit, in union with God, and the laws that govern the spirit realm.

> *We are heirs of God and joint heirs with Christ.*

We are in this world but are not of it. By faith, we operate in the realm of the spirit the same way God does.

How can we do this? By taking what The Word says about us seriously. We must see ourselves the way God sees us—in Christ.

# Practice Seeing Yourself as God Sees You

**FOCUS:** "There is none righteous, no, not one.... For he hath made him to be sin for us, who knew no sin; that we might be made the righteousness of God in him" (Romans 3:10; 2 Corinthians 5:21).

> *We are in this world but we are not of it.*

Second Corinthians 5:21 says we are the righteousness of God in Christ. Righteousness is right-standing with God. It is not right conduct.

No one is able to conduct himself in such a manner as to deserve to be in right-standing with God (Romans 3:10).

We receive our righteousness by faith in the substitutionary sacrifice of the Lord Jesus Christ. He was made to be sin, that we might be made the righteousness of God in Him. Jesus gave up His right-standing with God so He could pay the penalty for our separation from God.

When God was satisfied that the price had been paid, He raised Jesus from the dead and received Him back into right-standing with Him. Because He did, righteousness has come upon all men (Romans 5:18). It is a free gift. We receive it by faith in the written Word.

*You are what The Word says
you are. You can do what The
Word says you can do.*

## Now Begin Enjoying It

Because you are in Christ, God sees you through the Cross of Calvary—totally separated from the bondage of Satan. He sees you as His child. Receive it by faith and speak what The Word says about you. Actively seek after the realm of God and the spiritual laws which govern that realm. You will continually walk in the blessings of God.

## *Message 1 Outlined*

I.  Seek first the kingdom of God and His righteousness
    A.  Do not seek after the things of this world

II. The kingdom of God is the realm of God
    A.  It is God Himself
    B.  It is the spiritual laws that govern that realm
        (Romans 8:2)
    C.  Luke 12:30-32: It is the Father's good pleasure to
        reveal that realm to us
    D.  We are joint heirs of this kingdom with Jesus
        (Romans 8:17)

III. His righteousness—which is by faith in the sacrifice of the
     Cross (2 Corinthians 5:21)
    A.  Because Jesus has paid the price, righteousness has
        come upon all men (Romans 5:18)
    B.  Righteousness is right-standing with God, not right
        doing

IV. It is God's will for us
    A.  To own the kingdom
    B.  Be delivered from this present evil world
        (Galatians 1:4)
    C.  To walk in the likeness of Christ (Galatians 4:19;
        Romans 8:29) enjoying the privileges of our right-
        standing with God

*Study Questions*

*(1) What is the kingdom of God?*

_____

_____

_____

*(2) Is it God's will for us to experience life in the kingdom of God?*

_____

_____

_____

*(3) What does it mean to be in this world but not of it?*

_____

_____

_____

_____

*(4) What is the righteousness of God?*

_____

_____

_____

_____

*(5) How do we receive His righteousness?*

_____

_____

_____

_____

## Study Notes

"For he hath made him to be sin for us, who knew no sin; that we might be made the righteousness of God in him."

2 Corinthians 5:21

## 2

*"They which receive abundance of grace and of the gift of righteousness shall reign in life by...Jesus Christ."*

Romans 5:17

There is no room for fear in the
heart of a believer who is meditating
on the love God has toward him.
This is a righteousness consciousness.

## MESSAGE TWO
### Seek First the Kingdom II

# Awareness of
# Your Right-Standing
# Leaves No Room for Fear...

*D*eveloping a righteousness consciousness is a major part of what Jesus was speaking about in Matthew 6:33.

# Reign in Life by Awareness of Your Right-Standing

*✐* **FOCUS:** "For if by one man's offence death reigned by one; much more they which receive abundance of grace and of the gift of righteousness shall reign in life by one, Jesus Christ" (Romans 5:17).

A righteousness consciousness is a state of being aware of your right-standing with God.

Romans 5:17 tells us that through Adam's offense, death (separation from God) reigned over all men. But, *much more* than death is the right to reign in life through the gift of righteousness.

The Apostle Paul was telling the Christians at Rome that the work God did through the Cross has greater power than the work Satan did through Adam's high treason.

Through the grace of God, righteousness is a free gift. By faith in Jesus Christ, our separation from God is nullified and we come into right-standing with Him. Nothing can separate us, now, from the love of God when we are in Christ Jesus (Romans 8:31-39).

> *Our righteousness is because God has chosen not to hold sin against us!*

Our righteousness is not because we have done something to deserve it. It is because God has chosen not to hold sin against us! *✐*

# Walk in a Love
# the World Cannot Ignore

**FOCUS:** "And the glory which thou gavest me I have given them; that they may be one, even as we are one: I in them, and thou in me, that they may be made perfect in one; and that the world may know that thou hast sent me, and hast loved them, as thou hast loved me" ( John 17:22-23).

Before He faced His trial and the cross, Jesus prayed for His disciples and for those who believe in Him because of their preaching. This prayer is recorded in John 17.

> *John 17:23 tells us God loves us with the same love that He loves Jesus.*

What Jesus prayed applies to every believer who is in Christ. You can read this chapter and *receive* everything that He prayed. You are a believer because you heard The Word of God, believed it in your heart and confessed His lordship in your life. Jesus was praying for *you.*

In verses 22-23, Jesus said we are one with Him and the Father. Through this union, we are also made one with each other. This oneness is to prove to the world that God loves us with the same love that He loves Jesus.

This fact cannot be understood with the natural mind. It can only be comprehended spiritually, by the power of the Holy Spirit. You will develop a righteousness consciousness by meditating on The Word concerning the love of God.

Because God so *loved* the world, He sent His only Son to be the world's substitute (John 3:16).

Through our faith in His sacrifice, we become His workmanship created in Christ Jesus (Ephesians 2:10).

"He did this that He might clearly demonstrate through the ages to come the immeasurable (limitless, surpassing) riches of His free grace (His unmerited favor) in kindness and goodness of heart toward us in Christ Jesus" (Ephesians 2:7, *Amplified Bible, Classic Edition*).

*Love was His motivation. God is love. In Christ Jesus you are in right-standing with God because He loves you. You are justified by faith and have peace with God.*

## Now Begin Enjoying It

Allow the Holy Spirit to paint an image on the inside of you by meditating on God's lovingkindness, His grace and His mercy toward you.

This is the righteousness which is of God. We are to seek this first. By meditating on this and building it into our consciousness, we will become "peace-with-God minded."

This awareness of right-standing builds our confidence in God's willingness to use His power in our behalf. We become *aware* of His love for us. And perfect love casts out fear (1 John 4:18).

There is no room for fear in the heart of a believer who is meditating on the love God has toward him. This is a righteousness consciousness.

$\mathcal{CD}$ 2 *Outlined*

I.  Righteousness is right-standing with God
    A.  We receive righteousness by faith (Romans 3:21-25, 5:17)

II. We are righteous because of God's love, because of who we are in Christ, not because of our conduct
    A.  God loves us as much as He loves Jesus (John 17:22-23; Ephesians 2:7)
    B.  We are His workmanship, created in Christ (Ephesians 2:10)
    C.  Build a righteousness consciousness through meditating on God's love for you

III. We are righteous because Jesus has paid the price, once and for all (Hebrews 10:14)
    A.  The blood of Jesus does not just cover sin, it remits sin and removes its power (Hebrews 10:1-2, 1:3, 10:17-18; 2 Corinthians 5:21; Hebrews 9:11-15)

## Study Questions

*(1) What is a righteousness consciousness?*

_____

_____

_____

*(2) Why are we the righteousness of God?*

_____

_____

_____

*(3) How is it possible to believe that God loves you with the same love that He loves Jesus?*

_____

_____

_____

*(4) Explain how you can develop righteousness consciousness.*

_____

_____

_____

*(5) What result or effect does right-standing with God have on your relationship with Him?*

_____

_____

_____

# Study Notes

"For God so loved the world, that he gave his only begotten Son, that whosoever believeth in him should not perish, but have everlasting life."

John 3:16

# 3

*"All things that the
Father hath are mine:
therefore said I, that
[the Holy Spirit] shall
take of mine, and shall
show it unto you."*

John 16:15

The Spirit of God will show you
how God sees you—
as if you've never sinned.

## MESSAGE THREE
### *Seek First the Kingdom III*

# Let the Holy Spirit
# Paint a Picture Inside You
# of the Real You

*A* righteousness consciousness
is the awareness a believer has of
his right-standing with God.
A sin consciousness is a sense of
unworthiness and guilt because of
separation from God.

# You Are Right to Be Conscious of Right-Standing

**FOCUS:** "Therefore being justified by faith, we have peace with God through our Lord Jesus Christ" (Romans 5:1).

As believers in union with Christ, we have the right to have a righteousness consciousness. The Cross of Calvary gives us this right.

Jesus has offered one sacrifice for sins. He is now seated at the right hand of God expecting His enemies to be made His footstool.

The purpose for Jesus' coming to redeem mankind and earth was to destroy the works of the devil (1 John 3:8). The Cross spoiled Satan's principalities and powers (Colossians 2:15).

In purging our sin, Jesus has not only delivered us from the sin nature but also cleansed us from the guilt of sin.

Since you have right-standing with God in Christ, you can approach Him without a sense of unworthiness or condemnation. By meditating in The Word where righteousness is concerned, the Holy Spirit can build a righteousness consciousness in you.

> *The Cross gives us the right to have a righteousness consciousness.*

Jesus said that it was more expedient for us that He should go away, for if He went to the Father, He would send us the Holy Spirit.

The Holy Spirit takes the things of God and reveals them to us (John 16:7, 13-16). The Spirit of God will paint a clear picture in your consciousness showing you how God sees you—as if you've never sinned. "Therefore being justified by faith, we have peace with God through our Lord Jesus Christ" (Romans 5:1).

# You Died With Him, Now He Lives Through You

**FOCUS:** "Now if we be dead with Christ, we believe that we shall also live with him" (Romans 6:8).

In Christ we have peace with God. We have been given rights and privileges in Him. When we are born again, we become the righteousness of God in Christ (2 Corinthians 5:17, 21).

> *Jesus said that we would do the works He did and even greater.*

We receive His nature and His ability. We were crucified with Christ, now Christ is living His life through us (Galatians 2:20).

Through the renewing of our minds to the Word, He will become fully formed in us (Romans 12:2; Galatians 4:19). Jesus said that we would do the works He did (John 14:12) and even greater. It is His power working through us.

He is the Head, we are His Body.

Satan is under our feet. He has no right to rule over the Body of Christ. We have been delivered from his authority.

As the righteousness of God in Christ, we have the privilege and the responsibility of standing fearlessly against Satan and all his cohorts, lording it over them, not being lorded over by them.

*The awareness of your right-standing with God will give you confidence toward Him. Believing Him to meet your needs will no longer be a struggle.*

A righteousness consciousness will cause you to be bold to use the authority of His Name to cast out the devil. You will not feel unworthy to speak His Name. You will expect God's power to work when you pray, just as Jesus expected it.

## Now Begin Enjoying It

You are a joint heir with Him. Taking your rightful place as a joint heir will cause you to bear much fruit. Your life will glorify God the Father (John 15:8).

ℳ *e s s a g e*  3  𝒪 *u t l i n e d*

I.  Righteousness consciousness—awareness of having right-standing with God
  A.  Sin consciousness—sense of unworthiness and guilt because of sin
  B.  The Cross gives us the right to a righteousness consciousness (Hebrews 10:14; 2 Corinthians 5:17-21)
    1.  Jesus bridged the gap between God and man (1 Timothy 2:5-6; Colossians 2:15)
    2.  We are not only cleansed of the sin but of the guilt of the sin (Hebrews 1:3, 10:1-2)

II.  Allow the Holy Spirit to build a righteousness consciousness through meditation in The Word concerning your right-standing with God (Romans 12:2; John 16:7, 13-16)

III.  Take advantage of your place in Christ
  A.  Put Satan underfoot (Hebrews 10:1; John 14:12; Romans 5:17-19)
  B.  Use the authority of Jesus' Name (Mark 16:17)
  C.  Have confidence in God

## Study Questions

*(1) Why was Jesus manifested in the earth?*

_____

_____

_____

*(2) How has the Cross of Calvary delivered us from the guilt of sin?*

_____

_____

_____

*(3) How were Satan and his works put under our feet as the Body of Christ?*

_____

_____

_____

*(4) Why was it more expedient for us that Jesus go back to the Father?*

_____

_____

_____

*(5) How will a righteousness consciousness affect your prayer life?*

_____

_____

_____

_____

## Study Notes

*"For he hath made him to be sin for us, who knew no sin; that we might be made the righteousness of God in him."*
2 Corinthians 5:21

## 4

*"I am crucified with Christ:
nevertheless I live; yet not I, but
Christ liveth in me: and the life
which I now live in the flesh I live
by the faith of the Son of God, who
loved me, and gave himself for me. I
do not frustrate the grace of God:
for if righteousness come by the law,
then Christ is dead in vain."*

Galatians 2:20-21

How far will our right-standing with God take us?

How much do we dare believe?

## MESSAGE FOUR
### Seek First the Kingdom IV

# Receive With Humility...
# Believe Without Limits

*B*rother Copeland asks us the questions, "How far will our right-standing with God take us? How much do we dare believe?"

# Take the Dare
# All Things Are Possible...

**FOCUS:** "If thou canst believe, all things are possible to him that believeth" (Mark 9:23).

By remaining humble before God and staying out of the area of pride, the righteousness of God will take you as far as your faith will dare to go. True humility is simply saying what God says about you and receiving it.

The Holy Spirit has been given to us to teach us how to operate in the righteousness of God. He is committed to revealing The Word to us when we humble ourselves and believe it. It is God's desire that our lives bear fruit and glorify Him.

We must, in true humility, receive the fact that God has given us His righteousness through the sacrifice of Jesus Christ. It is not something we can do for ourselves. But, by believing in our right-standing, through God's grace, we will be able to walk in the fullness of God and glorify Him.

> *The righteousness of God gives you access to His power.*

# Forget What God
# Has Forgotten

**FOCUS:** "Therefore if any man be in Christ, he is a new creature: old things are passed away..." (2 Corinthians 5:17).

> *See yourself the way God sees you—IN CHRIST.*

The Apostle Paul stood on his right-standing with God. So much so that, at one point, he wrote, "Receive us; we have wronged no man..." (2 Corinthians 7:2).

Before he was born again, this man was Saul, a devout Jew who persecuted the Christians. Obviously, he wronged many. But Saul died on the road to Damascus. He received Jesus as his Lord and Savior and became a new creature—old things passed away and all things became new!

Saul was crucified with Christ (Galatians 2:20) and became the righteousness of God in Him. He developed a righteousness consciousness and was able to forget his sins because he knew that God had forgotten them (Hebrews 10:17). Paul's confidence was in the cross—the Lord Jesus and Him crucified.

Paul humbled himself to receive the righteousness of God, by faith. God exalted him and commissioned him to write two-thirds of the New Testament. His letters to the churches give us the revelation of who we are in Christ.

You can develop a righteousness consciousness by meditating in these letters. See yourself the way God sees you—IN CHRIST.

*God wants you to
draw close to Him, humbly and
with a sense of belonging.*

## Now Begin Enjoying It

"Let us draw near with a true heart in full assurance of faith, having our hearts sprinkled from an evil conscience, and our bodies washed with pure water" (Hebrews 10:22).

You can come boldly to the throne of grace, expecting to find help in a time of need. Your conscience can be free from the guilt of sin. God forgets your sins and iniquities when you confess them. He cleanses you of all unrighteousness (1 John 1:9).

You can obtain and maintain your right-standing with God through the high priestly ministry of Jesus. The righteousness of God gives you access to the very power of the living God. All things are possible to you because of Him.

## *Message 4 Outlined*

I.   Right-standing with God
   A.   Righteousness produces power; the danger in this power is pride
      1.   True humility is simply saying and believing what God says about you
   B.   The Holy Spirit is available to teach you who you are in Christ

II.  You are the righteousness of God in Christ (2 Corinthians 5:21)
   A.   Because of the sacrifice of Christ, no more sacrifices are necessary (Hebrews 10:12-14)
      1.   You have access to God (Hebrews 10:19-22, 4:16)
   B.   Take advantage of your right-standing; example: the Apostle Paul (2 Corinthians 7:1-2)
      1.   You were crucified with Christ (Galatians 2:20)
      2.   You have access to the throne of God and His power
      3.   All things are possible (Mark 9:23)

# Study Questions

(1) What is true humility?

_____

_____

_____

(2) Why is it humble to say, "I am the righteousness of God in Christ"?

_____

_____

_____

(3) How could the Apostle Paul have the boldness to say, "We have wronged no man," when he had persecuted the Church?

_____

_____

_____

(4) How can you be cleansed of all unrighteousness when you have sinned?

_____

_____

_____

(5) How has the knowledge of your right-standing with God affected you personally?

_____

_____

_____

## Study Notes

"If we confess our sins, he is faithful and just to forgive us our sins,
and to cleanse us from all unrighteousness."
*1 John 1:9*

**5**

*"Ye also, as lively stones, are built up a spiritual house, an holy priesthood, to offer up spiritual sacrifices, acceptable to God by Jesus Christ."*

1 Peter 2:5

As lively stones, we not only offer the sacrifice of praise, but by the common bond of God's love, we form a spiritual house.

---

**MESSAGE FIVE**

*Seek First the Kingdom V*

---

# You Are a Living Stone Building a House of Praise and Love

*A*s believers who are in Christ Jesus, we can make the decision to allow our rightful place in Christ to have its rightful place in our lives.

# As a Priest,
# Offer Up Spiritual Sacrifices

**FOCUS:** "Ye also, as lively stones, are built up a spiritual house, an holy priesthood, to offer up spiritual sacrifices, acceptable to God by Jesus Christ" (1 Peter 2:5).

We have seen from The Word of God that in Christ we are the righteousness of God, joint heirs with Jesus Christ, citizens of the kingdom of God, kings and priests in a royal priesthood. This is not our doing. It is what God has done through Christ.

> *By praising God, we take our rightful place as kings and priests.*

The Bible calls us lively, or living, stones which form a spiritual house. We are capable of offering spiritual sacrifices acceptable to God through Jesus Christ (1 Peter 2:5).

What sacrifice is there left to offer?

# Praise—the Sacrifice
# That Remains to Be Offered

**FOCUS:** "By him therefore let us offer the sacrifice of praise to God continually, that is, the fruit of our lips giving thanks to his name" (Hebrews 13:15).

We know that Jesus has offered Himself as the sacrifice for sin, once and for all. Hebrews 13:15 says we are to offer the sacrifice of praise to God continually. We offer our sacrifice of the fruit of our lips giving thanks for His sacrifice that has provided our total redemption—our restoration to God and complete deliverance from the bondage of Satan.

Jesus has spoiled the devil, his principalities and powers (Colossians 2:15). He is seated at the right hand of the Father, making intercession for the saints.

Jesus is the Head, we are His Body. Satan is under our feet. Praise stills the enemy and the avenger. When we offer the sacrifice of praise to God, Satan and his maneuvers against us are stopped.

By praising God, we are acknowledging Satan's defeat. We take our rightful place as kings and priests reigning in life through Christ.

*As living stones, we not only offer the sacrifice of praise, but we form a spiritual house.*

Just as mortar holds stones together in the natural, the common bond of love holds the spiritual house together. The unity of the spirit and the unity of the faith will come as each living stone makes the decision to love the brethren.

# Now Begin Enjoying It

The love of God and our praise of God produce an unseen force. This force is the power of God.

God's very presence inhabits the praises of His people (Psalm 22:3). Satan cannot stand in the presence of God.

Psalm 9:3 says, "When mine enemies are turned back, they shall fall and perish at thy presence." It says when, not if.

Our enemy's retreat and falling is a sure thing in the presence of God!

## Message 5 Outlined

I.   God has made us kings and priests unto Him (Revelation 1:6)

   A.   He has given us the kingdom, the power, the authority operate as His under-rulers in the earth

   B.   It is up to each member of the Body of Christ to make the decision to walk in the fullness of his right-standing with God

II.  Lively stones (1 Peter 2:1-5)

   A.   We are lively stones which build a spiritual house

   B.   We are capable of offering the sacrifice of praise, giving thanks to God for the ultimate sacrifice—the Cross of Calvary

     1.   Jesus has disarmed Satan of his weapons (Colossians 2:15)

   C.   Praise stills the enemy and the avenger (Psalm 8:2; Matthew 21:6)

   D.   The love of God, in each member, holds the lively stones together to make a spiritual house

     1.   The love toward our brethren will unite the Body of Christ

III. Love and praise

   A.   Produce the unseen force of God's power

   B.   Cause Satan to be turned back, fall and perish (Psalm 9:3)

# Study Questions

*(1) When will the Body of Christ be operating at the maximum of its potential as the righteousness of God in Christ?*

_____

_____

_____

*(2) What is the spiritual sacrifice that we can offer to God?*

_____

_____

_____

*(3) How do we acknowledge Satan's defeat?*

_____

_____

_____

*(4) When a believer is praising and glorifying God, it stops Satan. Why?*

_____

_____

_____

*(5) What is the spiritual mortar binding the lively stones which build the Body of Christ?*

_____

_____

_____

## Study Notes

"*Jesus said unto him, If thou canst believe,
all things are possible to him that believeth.*"
Mark 9:23

# 6

*"Having therefore, brethren,
boldness to enter into the holiest
by the blood of Jesus...
and having an high priest
over the house of God; let us
draw near with a true heart
in full assurance of faith...."*

Hebrews 10:19, 21-22

As we become more aware of our right-standing
with God, we will spend more time in
intimate fellowship with Him.

---

## MESSAGE SIX
### *Seek First the Kingdom VI*

---

# Right-Standing Opens
# the Door to the Fellowship
# You've Longed For

W hat is our primary purpose
in developing a righteousness
consciousness? It is so we will
respond to life as much
like Jesus as possible.

# You're Beginning to Show a Family Resemblance

**FOCUS:** "And be renewed in the spirit of your mind; and…put on the new man, which after God is created in righteousness and true holiness" (Ephesians 4:23-24).

As new creatures in Christ, we are God's workmanship created in righteousness and true holiness (Ephesians 4:21-24). We have been predestinated to be conformed to the image of Jesus Christ (Romans 8:29). We need to be renewed in the attitude of our minds (Romans 12:2). In so doing, we will humble ourselves to believe what God has said about us, and then walk in the light of it.

To respond to life the way Jesus did in His earthly ministry, we must think and act like Him.

Jesus knew He was in right-standing with the Father. He had the righteousness of God, the very nature of God, in His spirit. Jesus also knew this righteousness made Him one with the Father who was in Him (John 10:30, 17:21). Wherever Jesus went, the Father went. He had a righteousness consciousness.

> *God invites you to draw near.*

# Time With God Affects
# What You Say and Do

**FOCUS:** "The Son can do nothing of himself, but what he seeth the Father do: for what things soever he doeth, these also doeth the Son likewise" (John 5:19).

Because of His awareness of the presence of God with Him, Jesus walked in holiness.

Holiness is conduct in line with God's standards. God is holy. Jesus nurtured His holiness through continual fellowship with His Father.

Jesus said that "the Son is able to do nothing of Himself... but is able to do only what He sees the Father doing" (John 5:19, Amplified Bible, Classic Edition). He knew the Father—His thoughts, His ways, His attitudes, His standards for living and His love, Jesus knew everything about the Father through personal, intimate fellowship with Him.

*We have access to this*
*intimate fellowship in the very*
*presence of our heavenly Father.*
*It is a new and living way,*
*not going into an earthly tabernacle,*
*but entering into the very presence*
*of God's throne room.*

## Now Begin Enjoying It

Through the new birth, we have the same righteousness Jesus enjoys. As we become more conscious of this right-standing, we will spend more time in His presence.

God is inviting us to draw near to Him with a true heart, fully assured of our acceptance (Hebrews 10:19-22). As new creations, we are the temple of God.

As we renew our minds to this fact and take advantage of God's invitation, we will lay aside the weights that easily beset us.

Fellowshiping with God purifies and provokes us to true holiness.

*CD 6 Outlined*

I.  As new creatures in Christ, we are God's workmanship created in righteousness and true holiness (Ephesians 4:21-24)

II.  We must renew our minds to this fact so we can be conformed to the image of Christ (Romans 8:29, 12:2)
    A.  We are in right-standing with God
    B.  We are one with God (John 17:21)
    C.  We are the temple of God (1 Corinthians 3:16)

III.  Because of Jesus, we have access to the very throne of God, to fellowship with Him on an intimate, personal basis
    A.  Fellowhip will cause us to know Him
    B.  Fellowship purges us; causes holiness

IV.  A righteousness consciousness and true holiness
    A.  Will cause us to love the brethren
    B.  It will cause us to refuse to participate in anything which serves Satan
    C.  Motivates our every action and thought to glorify God

## Study Questions

*(1) What is the primary purpose for developing a righteousness consciousness?*

_____

_____

_____

*(2) How was Jesus able to do only that which He saw the Father do and say what He heard the Father say?*

_____

_____

_____

*(3) What are some of the benefits of personal fellowship with God?*

_____

_____

_____

*(4) What is true holiness?*

_____

_____

_____

*(5) List at least two benefits of having a righteousness consciousness.*

_____

_____

_____

## Study Notes

"*Let us draw near with a true heart in full assurance of faith, having our hearts sprinkled from an evil conscience, and our bodies washed with pure water.*"
*Hebrews 10:22*

# 7

*"Meditate [in the Word of God] day and night, that thou mayest observe to do according to all that is written therein: for then thou shalt make thy way prosperous, and then thou shalt have good success."*

Joshua 1:8

By seeking first the kingdom of God
and His righteousness through time in His Word,
you grow confident in His will and assure
the success of all God shows you to do.

## MESSAGE SEVEN
### *Seek First the Kingdom VII*

# Substitution Was Made…
# The Plan Is Clear

*T*he most important thing the Body of Christ can learn is that in the sight of God, they are in right-standing with Him because of what Jesus did at Calvary.

# The Key to Growing Awareness of Right-Standing

**FOCUS:** "Thou shalt meditate [in the Word of God] day and night" (Joshua 1:8).

The key to understanding what Jesus did for you at Calvary and to developing a righteousness consciousness is in the instruction God gave Joshua: "This book of the law [the Word of God] shall not depart out of thy mouth; but thou shalt meditate therein day and night, that thou mayest observe to do according to all that is written therein: for then thou shalt make thy way prosperous, and then thou shalt have good success [or deal wisely]" (Joshua 1:8).

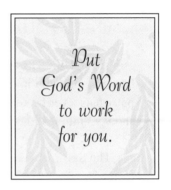

*Put God's Word to work for you.*

# Meditate on This: Jesus Was Made Sin for You

**FOCUS:** "[God] hath made him to be sin for us, who knew no sin; that we might be made the righteousness of God in him" (2 Corinthians 5:21).

A righteousness consciousness produces victory. We will experience the victory that Jesus won for us as we identify with His substitution. His substitution and our identification with it is the pivotal point of Christianity.

In building a righteousness consciousness, it is vital to know that Jesus was made to be sin for us. He never committed sin, but became the nature of sin so we could become His righteousness.

To the extent you realize Jesus was made to be sin, is how much you will see yourself as the righteousness of God in Him (2 Corinthians 5:21).

# Now You Have Access to the Plan…Work It

**FOCUS:** "Howbeit when he, the Spirit of truth, is come, he will guide you into all truth: for he shall not speak of himself; but whatsoever he shall hear, that shall he speak: and he will show you things to come" (John 16:13).

The Spirit of God has been sent to lead you into all truth (John 16:13). As you set your heart to receive from God, He will reveal His will to you. He will speak in your spirit, not into your physical ears.

> *Tune your spiritual ears to the Spirit of God.*

Put your confidence in God's ability to speak to you in a way that you can understand. And by His Spirit, He will begin to unfold His plan for your life to you.

When you know you are following the guidance of the Holy Spirit, it will not be difficult to use your faith to stay on track when pressure comes. When you know the will of the Lord for your life, set it as your goal, and do not stray from it.

Dealing wisely in the affairs of life is available to anyone who will meditate and act on The Word of God. Develop a righteousness consciousness with your spiritual ears tuned to the Spirit of God to lead and guide you wisely.

*Seeking first the kingdom of God and His righteousness will cause you to find out the will of God for your life.*

Every member of the Body of Christ has a specific job to do. Christ has fitly joined the Body together. But it is held together, or compacted, by the effectual working of every part. It is your right and privilege to know what your part is.

## Now Begin Enjoying It

Separate yourself from the things of this world and enter into the presence of God. Fellowship with Him and allow the eyes of your understanding to be enlightened through the power of the Holy Spirit.

By meditating The Word day and night, you will observe to act like you are the righteousness of God in Christ. It will cause you to make your way prosperous and have good success.

Anytime you meditate on The Word and put it to work in your life, it will cause you to prosper and succeed.

*Message* 7 *Outlined*

I. Because of Jesus, the kingdom of God is available to mankind (Colossians 1:12-14)
   A. Substitution and identification
      1. Jesus was our substitute; as a result, we identify with what we are in Him

II. Develop a righteousness consciousness
   A. Meditate in The Word day and night (Joshua 1:8)
   B. Righteousness consciousness produces victory

III. Seeking first the kingdom of God and His righteousness will produce:
   A. Your necessary food, clothes, shelter, your needs being met
   B. Your knowledge of God's will for your life

## Study Questions

*(1) What is the most important thing the Body of Christ can learn?*

_____

_____

_____

*(2) What is the pivotal point of all Christianity?*

_____

_____

_____

*(3) What does a righteousness consciousness produce?*

_____

_____

_____

*(4) How can you determine the will of God for your life?*

_____

_____

_____

*(5) How is the Body of Christ being held together?*

_____

_____

_____

_____

## Study Notes

"*In whom we have redemption through his blood,*
*even the forgiveness of sins.*"
Colossians 1:14

## 8

*"The work of righteousness shall be peace; and the effect of righteousness quietness and assurance for ever."*

Isaiah 32:17

No one can successfully be your foe
and nothing can prevail against you,
when you stand firmly on your
right-standing with God.

## MESSAGE EIGHT
### *Developing a Victory Consciousness*

## God Is for You...
## Who Can Be Against You?

*T*he new creation in Christ—the
born-again believer—is God's
most prized possession.

# God Is Utterly Interested in and Protective of His Family

**FOCUS:** "…I will dwell in them, and walk in them; and I will be their God, and they shall be my people" (2 Corinthians 6:16).

By making us the righteousness of God through Calvary, God has brought us into right-standing with Himself. He has cleansed us of sin.

God's nature is love. He desired a family and originally created man so that He *could* have a family. But then Adam sinned and severed the relationship between God and man. But in redeeming man, God has again made us sons and daughters through His Son Jesus. He is our Father, we are His family, reborn because of His love. He is so utterly interested in everything about us that He has become one with us.

> *God's nature is love. He desired a family.*

# God Is on Your Side—You Have Nothing to Fear

**FOCUS:** "…If God be for us, who can be against us?" (Romans 8:31).

As you consider the lengths God went to in order to restore you to fellowship with Him, you can see how much He is on your side.

Romans 8:31 is speaking of the fact that God has justified

us when it asks, "...If God be for us, who can be against us?"

No one can successfully be your foe when God is on your side. It doesn't matter how big the circumstances look, nothing can prevail against you when you stand firmly on your right-standing with God.

David slew the giant Goliath, not because he saw himself able, but because he saw God on his side. He knew he was in right-standing with God and that God was for him.

The effect of righteousness is quietness and assurance (Isaiah 32:17). Luke 1:74 says that we have been delivered from our foes that we might serve and love God without any fear of our enemy, Satan.

You can be confident of God's willingness to use His power in your behalf because of your right-standing with Him. You have no need to fear what Satan or man can do to you.

# God Always Moves on Behalf of Those in Right-Standing

**FOCUS:** "The eyes of the Lord are upon the righteous, and his ears are open unto their cry" (Psalm 34:15).

Through the Cross, God has accepted you as His very own child. He has given you rights in the kingdom of God and access to the entire ministry of Jesus. Jesus is your Lord. He is your Brother. You are a joint heir with Him. God loves you as much as He loves Jesus. You have as much right to expect God to move in your behalf as He would for Jesus.

> *Confess your right-standing with God when you pray.*

Jesus lived by faith in God during His earthly walk. He was a man who

knew His covenant rights. When Jesus prayed, the power of
God was manifest because of His faith and because He was a
Son in right-standing with His Father.

God wants you to experience the benefits of your right-
standing with Him. It will cause you to walk free of every trial
that Satan brings your way.

*You will see the power of God
meet every need in your life because
Jesus is your Lord and
victory is yours!*

Every member of the Body of Christ has a specific job to
do. Christ has fitly joined the Body together. But it is held together, or compacted, by the effectual working of every part. It
is your right and privilege to know what your part is.

## Now Begin Enjoying It

As a born-again believer, confess your right-standing with
God when you pray. It will cause you to have confidence in
Him. Your faith will be free to operate unhindered by guilt or
condemnation.

Maintain the integrity of your heart with the Lord by being
totally honest with Him. Immediately repent and confess your
sin when you miss the mark (1 John 1:9).

*Message 8 Outlined*

I.   The new creation in Christ is the righteousness of God
     (2 Corinthians 5:17, 21)
    A.   Through Calvary, God has restored mankind to
          Himself
        1.   As born-again believers, we are His very own
               sons and daughters

II.  God is for us, who can be against us?
    A.   God has justified us (Romans 8:31)
    B.   No one can successfully remain our enemy
    C.   The effect of righteousness is the assurance that God
          is on our side

III. God loves us as much as He loves Jesus
    A.   We can expect Him to respond to our faith

## Study Questions

*(1) What comes as a result of seeking first the kingdom of God and His righteousness?*

_____

_____

_____

*(2) Why was David victorious against Goliath?*

_____

_____

_____

*(3) What is the effect of righteousness?*

_____

_____

_____

*(4) When can nothing prevail against you?*

_____

_____

_____

*(5) Meditate on what you have learned about your right-standing with God for a few moments. How have your attitudes changed since you began to develop a righteousness consciousness?*

_____

_____

_____

## Study Notes

"And the work of righteousness shall be peace; and the effect of
righteousness quietness and assurance for ever."
*Isaiah 32:17*

## 9

*" [God] raised him from the dead, and set him at his own right hand in the heavenly places...and hath put all things under his feet...."*

Ephesians 1:20, 22

*"But God, who is rich in mercy, for his great love wherewith he loved us... [has] made us sit together in heavenly places in Christ Jesus."*

Ephesians 2:4, 6

Jesus' victory is our victory!

## MESSAGE NINE

*Triumph of Righteousness*

# Three Triumphs Over Satan That Are Triumphs for You

*I*t is the will of God for us, as the righteousness of God in Christ, to reign as kings in life through Jesus Christ (2 Corinthians 5:21; Romans 5:17).

# Believers Rule!

*✐* **FOCUS:** "...For this purpose the Son of God was manifested, that he might destroy the works of the devil" (1 John 3:8).

God created man as His under-ruler to have dominion in the earth (Genesis 1:28; John 10:34; Psalm 82:6). Adam's high treason caused mankind to become spiritually subject to Satan. Satan became the god of this world (2 Corinthians 4:4).

> *Jesus came to take back what the devil had stolen.*

Man's fall separated him from God and gave Satan legal right to rule over mankind. But Jesus was manifest in the earth to take away that right and to destroy the works of the devil (1 John 3:8). Jesus triumphed over him in every area. *✐*

# Three Strikes—Satan Is Out!

*✐* **FOCUS:** "Forasmuch then as the children are partakers of flesh and blood, he also himself likewise took part of the same; that through death he might destroy him that had the power of death, that is, the devil; and deliver them who through fear of death were all their lifetime subject to bondage" (Hebrews 2:14-15).

# There Are Three Main Areas in Which Jesus Triumphed Over Satan

## The first was during His earthly ministry.

In each of the Gospels, we read how Jesus healed and delivered all who were oppressed of the devil. He healed diseases and cast out demons throughout His ministry.

The devil tried to have Jesus stoned and thrown off a cliff. But Jesus said, "The prince of this world [Satan] cometh, and hath nothing in me" (John 14:30). He said no one could take His life from Him. He laid it down of His own free will (John 10:17-18).

## The second area of Jesus' triumph is through the cross.

In submitting Himself to death at the cross of Calvary, Jesus triumphed over Satan. Through death, He destroyed him who had the power of death, Satan (Hebrews 2:14). Jesus made an open show of him in his own domain!

## The third area of victory over Satan is the new creation.

When a man receives Jesus as his Lord and Savior at the new birth, Satan's spiritual hold on that man is totally severed. Colossians 1:13 says, "Who [Jesus] hath delivered us from the power of darkness...." We have been set free!

How does the believer walk in the victory that is his through Christ?

By accepting his new identity as a son of God.

The Bible says we were crucified with Him (Galatians 2:20). We died with Him (Romans 6:6, 8).

Ephesians 2:5-6 says we were made alive and raised together with Him. We are seated with Christ in heavenly places, "far above all principality, and power, and might, and dominion, and every name that is named, not only in this world, but also in that which is to come" (Ephesians 1:21).

His victory is our victory!

*Jesus did not gain victory over Satan for Himself. He did it for us, to restore us to God. Jesus was made sin with our sinfulness that we could be made righteous with His righteousness. What God wrought in Jesus, He wrought in us.*

## Now Begin Enjoying It

God has given us everything we need to walk victoriously in this life. We have His nature, His armor, His power, His Spirit, His Name, His Word and the authority to use them for His purposes in the earth.

## *Message 9 Outlined*

I.   Jesus was our substitute (2 Corinthians 5:14-21)
     A.   He took on Himself our sinfulness to give us His
          righteousness

II.  Jesus was manifest to destroy the works of the devil
     (1 John 3:8)

III. Jesus conquered Satan in three areas
     A.   During His earthly walk
     B.   Through Calvary
     C.   In the new creation

IV.  As new creatures in Christ, we share His victory by our
     identification with Him
     A.   Bondage to Satan is destroyed
     B.   Satan is rendered powerless or paralyzed where we
          are concerned
     C.   We died, were buried and raised together with Christ
          (Galatians 2:20; Romans 6:6, 8; Ephesians 2:5-6)
     D.   We are now seated with Him, spiritually, at the
          Father's right hand (Ephesians 1:21, 2:6)
          1.   We are victorious over Satan because Jesus is

## Study Questions

*(1) How do we know that God wants us to reign in life?*

_____

_____

_____

_____

*(2) List the three ways Jesus is victorious over Satan.*

_____

_____

_____

*(3) Why is His victory our victory?*

_____

_____

_____

_____

*(4) What has God given us to walk victoriously in this life?*

_____

_____

_____

_____

*(5) How does a man sever himself from Satan's hold on his life?*

_____

_____

_____

## Study Notes

"And hath raised us up together, and made us sit together
in heavenly places in Christ Jesus."
Ephesians 2:6

# 10

## "For the law of the Spirit of life in Christ Jesus hath made me free from the law of sin and death."

Romans 8:2

As citizens of the kingdom of God through our right-
standing, we have rights and privileges
bought and paid for by the blood of Jesus
and governed by spiritual laws.

## MESSAGE TEN
### The Law of Righteousness

# Put the Law of Faith to Work...
# Believe and Say

*A* law is a statement of an order or relation of facts that is invariable under the given conditions.

For example, the law of gravity is invariable under the conditions that regulate it. It can be superseded by other laws, but only under different conditions. As long as the conditions have been met, a law will work every time it is applied.

# Learn How to Make the Law of Faith Work for You

**FOCUS:** "Where is boasting then? It is excluded. By what law? of works? Nay: but by the law of faith" (Romans 3:27).

According to Romans 3:27, there is the law of faith. That means, when the conditions have been met, the law of faith will produce results.

As believers, we have been made the righteousness of God in Christ. It is a free gift from God to man.

> *Our righteousness is by faith in the blood of Jesus.*

Man cannot try to make himself righteous and then present himself worthy of a relationship with God without the new birth. No man is righteous in himself, for all have sinned and come short of the glory of God (see Romans 3:10, 23). Our righteousness is *by faith* in the blood of Jesus. We have been justified freely through God's *unmerited* favor.

# Believe in Your Heart and Say With Your Mouth

**FOCUS:** "That if thou shalt confess with thy mouth the Lord Jesus, and shalt believe in thine heart that God hath raised him from the dead, thou shalt be saved. For with the heart man believeth unto righteousness; and with the mouth confession is made unto salvation" (Romans 10:9-10).

We receive our right-standing with God by applying the law of faith. The conditions of the law of faith are set forth in Romans 10:9-10. The conditions are to: 1) *believe in your heart* and *say with your mouth* that you accept the sacrifice of Calvary that payed your sin debt  and gave you right-standing with God, and 2) confess the lordship of Jesus in your life.

The Bill of Rights is a statement of the rights of cititzens of the United States. As citizens of the kingdom of God, through our right-standing with Him, we have rights and privileges. The New Testament is a statement of those rights.

These rights were bought and paid for by the blood of Jesus Christ. There are laws that govern them. The Holy Spirit has been sent to lead us into all truth. It is His function to see to it that we understand these laws in order to put them to work here on earth.

*You have been given right-standing with God. You have been given the rights and privileges of a citizen of the kingdom of God. This does not just mean going to heaven when you die.*

# Now Begin Enjoying It

The law of the Spirit of life in Christ Jesus has delivered you from the law of sin and death (Romans 8:2). This law functions under the same conditions as the law of faith.

By *believing in your heart* and speaking with your mouth Romans 8:2, the Holy Spirit will see to it that you are delivered from fear, sickness, poverty, evil men, etc.—everything that constitutes the law of sin and death.

You will *believe in your heart* when you have meditated The Word enough for the Holy Spirit to paint a clear image in your consciousness that you are the righteousness of God in Christ. This clear image will dispel all doubt and fear and you will be able to act like what you are—the righteousness of God.

$\mathcal{M}$ *essage 10* $\mathcal{O}$ *utlined*

I.  A law: a statement of an order or relation of facts that is invariable under given conditions
    A.  Example: law of gravity

II. Faith is a law (Romans 3:27)
    A.  The conditions are
        1.  Believing with the heart
        2.  Confessing with the mouth (Romans 10:9-10)
    B.  Righteousness (right-standing with God) is by faith (Romans 3:20-26)
        1.  Jesus was our substitute, therefore we have a right to enjoy the benefits of Calvary
        2.  The law of the Spirit of life has made you free from the law of sin and death (Romans 8:2)
            a.  Activated by the law of faith
    C.  Spiritual laws work when the conditions are met

III. Right-standing with God gives the believer rights and privileges in Christ
    A.  To be delivered from this present evil world (Galatians 1:4) and the law of sin and death
    B.  To be a joint heir with Jesus (Romans 8:17)
    C.  To have the power of God manifest in your life (Ephesians 1:19)
    D.  To enjoy abundant life (John 10:10)
    E.  E. To enjoy fellowship with God the Father, Jesus Christ, and our fellow believers (1 John 1:3)

## *S t u d y   Q u e s t i o n s*

*(1) Explain the meaning of a law as it is used in this message.*

_____

_____

_____

*(2) What are the conditions for the law of faith to produce results?*

_____

_____

_____

*(3) Explain what is truly meant in Romans 3:10, 23.*

_____

_____

_____

*(4) How does the Christian believe with his heart?*

_____

_____

_____

*(5) List some of your rights as a citizen in the kingdom of God (see Hebrews 4:16; Philippians 4:19; 2 Peter 1:4; Galatians 3:13, 29).*

_____

_____

_____

_____

## Study Notes

"*For with the heart man believeth unto righteousness; and with the mouth confession is made unto salvation.*"

Romans 10:10

## 11

*"For out of the abundance of the heart the mouth speaketh. A good man out of the good treasure of the heart bringeth forth good things...."*

Matthew 12:34-35

By meditating it and building an inner image of The Word, then speaking it, you can control your body, your circumstances, everything that concerns your life.

## MESSAGE ELEVEN
### The Bible Secret of Words

## Words Build Inner Images…
## What Pictures Are You Painting?

*T*here is a Bible secret to the words
of your mouth. To understand this,
read James 2:22-26, 3:1-18.

# You Will Produce What You Store in Your Heart

**FOCUS:** "...Out of the abundance of the heart the mouth speaketh. A good man out of the good treasure of the heart bringeth forth good things: and an evil man out of the evil treasure bringeth forth evil things" (Matthew 12:34-35).

Words build inner images. When you hear the word "dog" you do not think D-O-G. You instantly picture a dog in your mind. It is your dog, your neighbor's dog or some dog that you have seen before. So words form pictures, not alphabetical letters, in your mind.

> *Words build inner images.*

Inner images are fundamental. Man is a creative being. He will *produce* whatever he has pictured in his heart.

Jesus said that an evil man, out of the evil treasure of his heart, will produce evil things. And a good man, out of the good treasure of his heart, will produce good things. The treasure is what he puts in his heart in abundance, or what he thinks about continually.

Jesus said that *out of the abundance of the heart the mouth speaks.*

# Build an Inner Image Based on What God Says

**FOCUS:** "For I know the thoughts and plans that I have

for you, says the Lord, thoughts and plans for welfare and peace and not for evil, to give you hope in your final outcome" (Jeremiah 29:11, *Amplified Bible, Classic Edition*).

God's Word is His will for your life.

You can stop Satan's plots and plans against you by The Word of God. By meditating it and building an inner image of The Word, *then speaking it,* you can control your body, your circumstances and everything that concerns your life.

When you learn to control your tongue you will be able to control the course of your life. The words of your mouth set on fire the course of nature. They can create a world of iniquity or they can destine you to follow God's plan for your life.

This is why the Bible places such a high priority on the words of your mouth.

"For I know the thoughts and plans that I have for you, says the Lord, thoughts and plans for welfare and peace and not for evil, to give you hope in your final outcome" (Jeremiah 29:11, *Amplified Bible, Classic Edition*).

*There are two kinds of wisdom available to us. Natural man's wisdom does not come from God. It is earthly, sensual and devilish. But the wisdom of God…is first pure, then peaceable, gentle, and easy to be entreated, full of mercy and good fruits, without hypocrisy (James 3:17).*

As we seek after the wisdom of God, which is His Word, and form an inner image of it and speak it, God can take those words and bring to pass His plans for our welfare and peace.

## Now Begin Enjoying It

The Bible says that a fountain cannot give sweet and bitter water.

Our mouths should not speak blessing and cursing. You can bless God and everyone else around you with the words of your mouth. This takes your spirit man to be in ascendancy over your mind and body.

By meditating and speaking only The Word, your spirit will dominate. It takes spiritual power to control your tongue. It begins with a quality decision.

The Holy Spirit is your Helper. Put your confidence in Him and be quick to obey His leading in your heart. You will experience the victory that is available to you!

*Message 11 Outlined*

I.  Man is a creative being
    A.  He produces what he thinks in his heart (Matthew 12:34-36) or what he meditates on
        1.  Words build images
        2.  The mouth speaks what is in the heart in abundance

II.  God desires to perform His will in your life, but He needs the words of your mouth
    A.  The tongue is like the helm of a ship; it steers your life
    B.  God's Word is His will for you; by disciplining your tongue to speak God's Word, it will direct your life in the course of His plan
    C.  Make a *quality* decision to control your tongue with The Word of God; speak *only The Word*

III.  A fountain cannot give sweet *and* bitter water; the mouth cannot speak blessing *and* cursing
    A.  Meditate on The Word; control your thoughts and words by keeping God's Word in your heart in abundance
    B.  You will bless God, your family and your neighbors with the words of your mouth

## *Study Questions*

*(1) Why are inner images so important?*

_____

_____

_____

*(2) Explain why the Bible places such a high priority on the words of your mouth.*

_____

_____

_____

*(3) Find as many scriptures as you can on the words of your mouth.*

_____

_____

_____

*(4) How can you control the course of your life to follow God's plan for you?*

_____

_____

_____

*(5) How does the Bible describe the wisdom that is from God?*

_____

_____

_____

## Study Notes

"And the fruit of righteousness is sown in peace
of them that make peace."
James 3:18

## 12

*"The thief cometh not,
but for to steal, and to kill,
and to destroy: I am come
that they might have life,
and that they might have
it more abundantly."*

John 10:10

Once you realize that all tests, trials and temptations
come from Satan and not God, you can begin to
resist your real enemy, and he must flee.

## MESSAGE TWELVE
### *The Troublemaker*

# Identify and Resist the Troublemaker...He Has to Flee

*T*he Body of Christ is coming to the place of being single-minded on The Word of God. We must know who our enemy is so that we can successfully resist him.

# No Substitute Teachers

✍ **FOCUS:** "…If ye continue in my word, then are ye my disciples indeed; And ye shall know the truth, and the truth shall make you free" (John 8:31-32).

The belief that tests and trials come into our lives as tools that God uses to teach us and strengthen us is a lie. The Holy Spirit has been sent as the Teacher of the Church. He is here to lead us into all truth. God uses His Word and the Holy Spirit to teach us.

Where do the temptations, tests and trials come from?

John 10:10 says that Satan is the one who comes to steal, kill and destroy.

If a man believes in any way that God is the One who is behind his trouble, he will not resist it. The Bible says if we resist Satan, he will flee from us (James 4:7). ✍

> *If we resist Satan, he will flee.*

# What the Devil Is Really After— God's Word in Your Heart

✍ **FOCUS:** "…But when they have heard, Satan cometh immediately, and taketh away the word that was sown in their hearts" (Mark 4:15).

Mark 4 tells us that the reason Satan comes is to take away The Word that has been sown in a man's heart (Mark 4:15). The devil has no defense against the things of God, when they are properly being used.

God has given the Body of Christ His Spirit, His armor, authority in the Name of Jesus, His own resurrection power and The Word of God that we might successfully stand against the wiles of the devil.

To understand this, you need to know that it was this way for Adam in the Garden of Eden. He had the nature of God. He was a free moral agent with the right to his own choices. And He was given the authority to have dominion as God's under-ruler in the earth.

God had given His Word to Adam. He told him to have dominion over the earth. When Adam disobeyed God, he turned his authority over to Satan who became the god of this world (2 Corinthians 4:4).

# Where Jesus and Satan Crossed Paths Concerning You

**FOCUS:** "[The Father] hath delivered us from the power of darkness, and hath translated us into the kingdom of his dear Son" (Colossians 1:13).

> *The devil has no defense against the things of God.*

When Jesus went to the cross, He delivered us from the power of darkness and translated us into the kingdom of God. The Cross is where you rightly divide the truth.

At Calvary, Jesus took the chastisement by punishment that was rightfully due us (Isaiah 53:4-5). He became a curse to redeem us from the curse (Galatians 3:13; Deuteronomy 28:16-68).

Jesus bore every sickness, disease, weakness, sorrow, pain

and distress—everything that Satan could inflict on a man. Jesus took them on Himself to redeem us from them. He has delivered us from the authority Satan took from man at the Fall.

Jesus has restored man to his rightful place. Man is reconciled to God.

When the believer walks in the confidence of his redemption, Satan has no defense. He brings tests and trials your way to steal The Word before it has a chance to become rooted in your heart.

> *God, however, has said "No weapon that is formed against thee shall prosper..."*
> *(Isaiah 54:17).*

Jesus said the one who is a doer of The Word is like a man who digs deep and lays the foundation of his house on a rock. The storms of life cannot shake it.

The man who hears The Word but does not do it or continue in it, is like the one who builds his house on the sand. The storms cause it to fall immediately (Luke 6:47-49). He is not rooted deeply in The Word.

## Now Begin Enjoying It

Your foundation must be The Word. Decide today that you will never allow Satan to steal from you again. The choice is yours (Deuteronomy 30:19).

*Message 12 Outlined*

I.   Source of temptations, tests and trials is Satan, not God (John 10:10; James 1:1-8, 13; Mark 4:15)

II.  God has provided a way of escape—the Cross
    A.   Jesus has delivered us (Colossians 1:13)
    B.   He has restored authority in His Name to the Church (Mark 16:15-20)
    C.   He has given us His Spirit to teach us (John 16:13)
    D.   He has given us His Word to correct, reprove, instruct, convict, train and discipline us (2 Timothy 3:16-17, *Amplified Bible, Classic Edition*)
    E.   He has given us His power (Ephesians 1:18-20) and the authority to use it (John 14:12; Luke 10:19)

III. The choice is ours (Deuteronomy 30:19)
    A.   It is up to *us* to resist Satan, and he will flee from us (James 4:7)
    B.   Victory is certain if we will continue in The Word

*Study Questions*

*(1) Who is the author of sickness, disease, temptations, tests and trials?*

_____

_____

_____

*(2) Why is it so important that the believer become single-minded on The Word of God?*

_____

_____

_____

*(3) Who is the Teacher of the Church?*

_____

_____

_____

*(4) How does God correct us?*

_____

_____

_____

*(5) Why must your foundation be in The Word?*

_____

_____

_____

## Study Notes

"*That ye might walk worthy of the Lord unto all pleasing, being fruitful in every good work, and increasing in the knowledge of God.*"
Colossians 1:10

# Prayer for Salvation and Baptism in the Holy Spirit

*Heavenly Father, I come to You in the Name of Jesus. Your Word says, "Whosoever shall call on the name of the Lord shall be saved" (Acts 2:21). I am calling on You. I pray and ask Jesus to come into my heart and be Lord over my life according to Romans 10:9-10: "If thou shalt confess with thy mouth the Lord Jesus, and shalt believe in thine heart that God hath raised him from the dead, thou shalt be saved. For with the heart man believeth unto righteousness; and with the mouth confession is made unto salvation." I do that now. I confess that Jesus is Lord, and I believe in my heart that God raised Him from the dead. I repent of sin. I renounce it. I renounce the devil and everything he stands for. Jesus is my Lord.*

*I am now reborn! I am a Christian—a child of Almighty God! I am saved! You also said in Your Word, "If ye then, being evil, know how to give good gifts unto your children: HOW MUCH MORE shall your heavenly Father give the Holy Spirit to them that ask him?" (Luke 11:13). I'm also asking You to fill me with the Holy Spirit. Holy Spirit, rise up within me as I praise God. I fully expect to speak with other tongues as You give me the utterance (Acts 2:4). In Jesus' Name. Amen!*

Begin to praise God for filling you with the Holy Spirit. Speak those words and syllables you receive—not in your own language, but the language given to you by the Holy Spirit. You have to use your own voice. God will not force you to speak. Don't be concerned with how it sounds. It is a heavenly language!

Continue with the blessing God has given you and pray in the spirit every day.

You are a born-again, Spirit-filled believer. You'll never be the same!

Find a good church that boldly preaches God's Word and obeys it. Become part of a church family who will love and care for you as you love and care for them.

We need to be connected to each other. It increases our strength in God. It's God's plan for us.

Make it a habit to watch the Believer's Voice of Victory Network and become a doer of the Word, who is blessed in his doing (James 1:22-25).

# About the Author

Kenneth Copeland is co-founder and president of Kenneth Copeland Ministries in Fort Worth, Texas, and best-selling author of books that include *Honor—Walking in Honesty, Truth and Integrity,* and *THE BLESSING of The LORD Makes Rich and He Adds No Sorrow With It.*

Since 1967, Kenneth has been a minister of the gospel of Christ and teacher of God's Word. He is also the artist on award-winning albums such as his Grammy-nominated *Only the Redeemed, In His Presence, He Is Jehovah, Just a Closer Walk* and *Big Band Gospel.* He also co-stars as the character Wichita Slim in the children's adventure videos *The Gunslinger, Covenant Rider* and the movie *The Treasure of Eagle Mountain,* and as Daniel Lyon in the Commander Kellie and the Superkids™ videos *Armor of Light* and *Judgment: The Trial of Commander Kellie.* Kenneth also co-stars as a Hispanic godfather in the 2009 and 2016 movies *The Rally* and *The Rally 2: Breaking the Curse.*

With the help of offices and staff in the United States, Canada, England, Australia, South Africa and Ukraine, Kenneth is fulfilling his vision to boldly preach the uncompromised WORD of God from the top of this world, to the bottom, and all the way around. His ministry reaches millions of people worldwide through daily and Sunday TV broadcasts, magazines, teaching audios and videos, conventions and campaigns, and the World Wide Web.

**When The LORD first spoke to Kenneth and Gloria Copeland about starting the *Believer's Voice of Victory* magazine...**

He said: *This is your seed. Give it to everyone who ever responds to your ministry, and don't ever allow anyone to pay for a subscription!*

For more than 50 years, it has been the joy of Kenneth Copeland Ministries to bring the good news to believers. Readers enjoy teaching from ministers who write from lives of living contact with God, and testimonies from believers experiencing victory through God's WORD in their everyday lives.

Today, the *BVOV* magazine is mailed monthly, bringing encouragement and blessing to believers around the world. Many even use it as a ministry tool, passing it on to others who desire to know Jesus and grow in their faith!

**Request your FREE subscription to the *Believer's Voice of Victory* magazine today!**

Go to **freevictory.com** to subscribe online, or call us at **1-800-600-7395** (U.S. only) or **+1-817-852-6000**.

# We're Here for You!®

Your growth in God's WORD and victory in Jesus are at the very center of our hearts. In every way God has equipped us, we will help you deal with the issues facing you, so you can be the **victorious overcomer** He has planned for you to be.

The mission of Kenneth Copeland Ministries is about all of us growing and going together. Our prayer is that you will take full advantage of all The LORD has given us to share with you.

Wherever you are in the world, you can watch the *Believer's Voice of Victory* broadcast on television (check your local listings), the Internet at kcm.org or on our digital Roku channel.

Our website, **kcm.org,** gives you access to every resource we've developed for your victory. And, you can find contact information for our international offices in Africa, Australia, Canada, Europe, Ukraine and our headquarters in the United States.

Each office is staffed with devoted men and women, ready to serve and pray with you. You can contact the worldwide office nearest you for assistance, and you can call us for prayer at our U.S. number, 1-817-852-6000, seven days a week!

We encourage you to connect with us often and let us be part of your everyday walk of faith!

Jesus Is LORD!

*Kenneth & Gloria Copeland*

Kenneth and Gloria Copeland